Reading Aloud
Is More Than
Reading Words

Reading Aloud Is More Than Reading Words

Judy Wolfman

Write My Wrongs, LLC, P.O. Box 80781 Lansing, MI 48908
United States
www.writemywrongsediting.com

Contents

INTRODUCTION

Reading aloud to students is certainly not a new concept, and in all probability, you already do it. If you're an early elementary teacher, you probably read several stories throughout the day. However, teachers of higher elementary grades, secondary school, and specialized subjects seem to have less time for reading aloud.

Besides validating the importance of reading aloud in the classroom, I offer several suggestions for reading aloud options (other than story books), as well as how and when to read aloud.

But my main intention in writing this book is to provide parents, grandparents, teachers, caregivers and anyone else who comes in contact with children with effective strategies for reading aloud, which is more than just reading words, as you will discover.

Now during the pandemic, many children are staying away from the classroom and being taught at home. These strategies make good sense to use in an effort to help children with their reading and comprehensive skills through reading aloud.

Although most of the information provided in this book refers to "the teacher", but if a child is being home schooled, the "teacher" is the parent, relative, caregiver, or some other adult.

After reading this book, I hope you will put these strategies to good use as you incorporate many read aloud opportunities.

Happy reading aloud!

Judy Wolfman

CHAPTER 1

What Is Reading Aloud and Who Does It?

"If we truly wish to revolutionize American education, we must put far more pleasure into the reading experience. And the most effective and time-honored way of doing that is by reading aloud to the child, the family, and the class," states Jim Trelease, author of *The Read Aloud Handbook* and advocate for reading aloud.

What is reading aloud? It is a planned oral reading of a book or print excerpt to one or more people. Reading aloud engages the student listener, while developing background knowledge, increasing comprehension skills and fostering critical thinking. In addition, reading aloud can be used to model the use of reading strategies that help students with their comprehension skills.

Up until about 8th grade, young people have a "listening level" that surpasses their reading level, so listening allows students to become engaged in material that they might not be able to read. Therefore, listening to someone reading aloud becomes preferable to reading silently.

Ideally, reading aloud begins at birth, when parents read to their newborn. What they read is not important, but the concept of rhythmic words coming from a book is. This is the child's first exposure to language and sets the stage for future reading.

Joining the parade of readers for children are grandparents, siblings, relatives, friends, babysitters and many other individuals who take the time to share a picture book with the young child. Each reader places another block on the foundation for reading, until eventually a strong building is constructed, and the young listener emerges into a young reader.

Unfortunately, not all children are read to at home in those formative years. Therefore, when the child enters school, the teacher assumes the role of reader, and faces many challenges. The child, unaccustomed to being read to, doesn't always know how to listen or respond to a story. In daycare and preschool programs, reading aloud is the core of the program - teachers enjoy reading stories, and children learn to love listening to them.

Teachers spend a lot of time and energy preparing children to listen, but eventually, as children develop listening skills, it becomes worthwhile.

It is said that children learn to read in grades K-2, and read to learn in grades 3 and up. Teachers in the early grades feel their primary job is to teach children <u>how</u> to read – sight recognition, phonetic approaches, being able to read a complete sentence or paragraph without stumbling over words, and so on.

Teachers no longer feel the strong need to read to their students. But what is overlooked is that reading aloud is a time of enjoyment and relaxation for both teachers and students – a time when powerful, effective teaching and rigorous learning can take place. It doesn't require a script or lesson plan to validate it – kids learn!

The "instructional" attitude becomes more pronounced in the upper grades, and specific areas of curriculum. This needs to be revisited! Research has shown that reading aloud gives students a sense of the language or print, thus enabling them to more readily figure out print on their own. Reading aloud has been touted as the single most important activity for building the knowledge and skills eventually required for success in reading.

Reading aloud is ongoing – it doesn't stop at graduation! It is a life-long skill that carries over into the professional world - when a CEO reads his report; when a lawyer reads his summary on behalf of a client; when a motivational speaker reads his notes to document his points.

Reading aloud is a form of communication in a family unit when a wife reads an excerpt from an article she wants to share with her husband; when a father reads directions to his son as they create a project together; when a theatrical agent reads a review to his client over the phone.

If reading aloud is so important in our daily lives, it must be developed during the school years. Many adolescents struggle with reading – either they cannot read; read, but not well; or read well, but do not study effectively and need help in processing text.

Many teachers faced with the challenges of teaching children how to read, find that their students develop, and use, the reading skills through reading aloud.

A small amount of time every day (10 – 15 min. per session) is all it takes! A wise investment that offers a high return!

CHAPTER 2

Why Read Aloud?

 few "generic" points were made on behalf of reading aloud in Chapter 1, but now let's look at some specific values of this approach to teaching reading.

<u>**Obvious Reasons for Reading Aloud**</u>

- To share a wonderful story.

- To relax and enjoy a story or reading.

- To share fascinating, interesting or unique information.

- To teach a needed skill or strategy.

- To make connections between content and the real world.

- Basic Values of Reading Aloud

- Reading aloud helps create a mentally healthy child.

- Exposes students to vocabulary and language patterns that are not part of their everyday speech.
- Introduces students to concepts, information, values, morals, discipline they may not otherwise discover on their own.
- Enhances listening and concentration skills.
- Encourages critical thinking skills.
- Develops comprehension skills, skills for solving problems, and decision-making.
- Stimulates and activates imagination and creativity.
- It's exciting, and takes students to places they wouldn't go to otherwise.
- Helps students share ideas, opinions and experiences as related to the text.
- Makes students aware of other cultures and people in the world.
- Helps students become aware of feelings such as empathy and love.
- Encourages students to connect reading aloud to previous experiences (text to text, text to self, text to the world).
- Allows a student to connect the reading aloud experience to small group and whole group instructions.
- Provides understanding that print has meaning – connects between the written and spoken word. Especially helpful with ESL students.
- Helps students become familiar with phrasing, expression, and flow of sentences for their own reading and writing.
- Prepares students to understand the structure of books when they read or write independently.
- Helps students learn how to pronounce words, and develop their own expressive interpretations and reading.

- Helps students deal with an increasingly sophisticated range of texts and reading materials.
- Helps students understand and appreciate literature.
- Motivates students to want to read, to read more deeply and to have joy while learning.
- Leads to good, productive adults.
- It's restful, relaxing, and entertaining!

Teacher as a Role Model

- All students need role models who are readers.
- By getting excited about books, taking time to read to students, and sharing their interest in books, teachers show the positive effects of reading and inspire students to read.
- Listening level is higher than reading level, so students can comprehend more difficult and interesting material.
- Reader's pauses and emphases let students to better understand the phrasing and fluency of the language.
- Hearing new words and the way they are used broadens vocabulary and allows for greater understanding.
- Teacher's interpretation helps students understand the story and characters better.
- Listening to the story allows students to develop key understanding and skills, and appreciate how the story is written.
- Strong modeling paves the way for future skilled, strong readers.
- Listening to story/text is more interesting and exciting than reading it independently.

- Teacher's skills motivate students to be expressive and skillful in reading aloud.
- As students follow along, they can match pauses with punctuation and structure of the written work.
- Provides a good forum for dialogue and interpretation, where reading aloud is more powerful, meaningful and entertaining – such as in Shakespeare.
- Show that we first need to learn to read; then read to learn.

The reasons for reading aloud vary from teacher to teacher, and from day to day. But, whatever the motive for reading aloud, the recommendation is to read <u>something</u> aloud every day for 10 – 15 minutes. When to do it is entirely up to the teacher.

CHAPTER 3

When to Read Aloud

I t's probably an understatement to say that teachers are busy people! Between planning lessons, taking notes, preparing handout materials, writing and correcting quizzes and exams, maintaining grades and reports, and hundreds of other daily chores too numerous to mention, teachers are constantly working!

So, when does a teacher have time to squeeze in a "reading aloud" opportunity?

Actually it's not as daunting as it may sound, and can range anywhere from a scheduled time to a spontaneous one.

The Scheduled Time

Perhaps a 10 – 15 minute time slot can be allocated each day to the reading (or partial reading) of a picture book or chapter book. If you're reading a continuing story, students look forward to hearing what happens next, but be sure to give a quick overview of where you left off the day before. This ensures continuity.

This time slot could also be used for reading more about a specific subject being studied – a culture, animal, era in history, scientific discovery, or whatever is currently in the plan for the day. Such information doesn't always have to be related as a lecture, or through the "read and discuss" method. Hearing the teacher read loud brings the subject to life.

It's advisable to try to stick to a scheduled time, one that the students will look forward to. However, sometimes that is easier said than done, so it's important to be flexible. A few minutes earlier or later won't hurt anything, but the important thing is that the reading aloud time is recognized and executed.

Although the recommended time frame for reading aloud is 10 – 15 minutes, it could vary depending upon what is being read. If it is intriguing and interesting, the reading aloud time could go on for several more minutes. If it is a short piece, it might only be 5 to 10 minutes.

If what you're reading is longer than you had planned for, or if your time runs short and you must cease, try to stop reading aloud at a logical point – one that will be a good place to begin the following day.

Spontaneous Read Aloud

At any time during the day, the teacher could "interrupt" the class with a one-liner, such as "Say, listen to this," or "I just read something interesting I think you might enjoy," or "What do you think about this?" There are many approaches for the interruption, but it should be one that is enthusiastic enough to encourage the students to stop what they're doing and listen.

The reading, although appearing to be spontaneous, is actually planned for by the teacher, but the timing is critical – when to provide the interruption, how to read the short material, and make sure it's relevant to what's going on in the classroom.

Once the material has been presented, it may generate a mini-discussion to allow the students to process what was read and express their feelings and thinking on it. A discussion is not mandatory, and if no one has anything to say, that is fine.

However, if it does evoke a discussion, which becomes too lengthy and involved, the teacher can express her pleasure at how this has stimulated the students, and suggest they talk about it at a later time. This would give the students an opportunity to think about it more, pull together their thoughts, and be prepared to express them in more depth later.

CHAPTER 4

What to Read Aloud

Reading aloud takes many forms, ranging from books (picture books, chapter books, novels, textbooks) to snippets from newspaper or magazine articles or excerpts from biographies or autobiographies. Actually, anything that is written can be read aloud. (Ever think about reading letters or diaries?) What is read aloud is often determined by the age of the listener and the intent for the reading aloud.

Reading instruction, which includes reading aloud, begins in Kindergarten and goes through 12th grade to produce the kinds of sophisticated readers we need for an information society.

Start Early

- There is no certain age at which to begin reading aloud, but the earlier the better! (This includes infants and toddlers, even though they have no working vocabulary yet.)

- Perhaps the first read aloud materials, designed for the very young child, are finger plays, rhymes, with repetitive words or phrases. The words may hold no meaning, but they flow and are like a gentle rhythm that is like music to a child. These can be read to several children at one time, and will become favorites as they are read again and again.

- Gradually, simple vocabulary words are introduced through colorfully illustrated board books, and as more words appear on the page, a brief, charming story unfolds with a simple plot and interesting characters.

- All, or most of these experiences, take place at home under the care of parents and/or relatives and caregivers.

Early Elementary Years

- For some children, where listening to stories is a new experience because reading aloud was not done at home, the classroom teacher needs to develop the child's interest and ability to listen to a story.

- Using a short, interesting story with strong pictures usually works well.

- Introducing easy reading books that the children enjoy encourages them to later reread the book on their own.

- On this level the child associates reading with warm, pleasant feelings, as he learns about words and language, so reading aloud several times during the day is beneficial.

- His listening skills build, and his vocabulary expands.

- He begins to talk about characters, the setting and plot, and relate the story to his own life – how to handle problems and cope with difficulties - while at the same time learning about new topics.

- These students are curious about their surrounding world – beyond their own experiences, so reading books that match their interests are important.

- Chapter books are popular, as the students get to know the characters, and relate to them, but enjoy hearing various plot twists and descriptive language.

- Eventually, the students seek the books to read independently.

- While reading to the students, teachers should scan their faces and body language to determine if the book is interesting or not. Being responsive to these "clues" enables the teacher to stop reading, and put the book aside. This is not a punishment, but more a recognition of "this is not working – I need to find something else."

- Students need to be aware, too, that not all books are for them and that choices can be made in selection.

- If the teacher has a good time reading aloud, chances are the children will enjoy the book, and the need to change is minimized. During and/or after reading, encourage a good discussion about the story – ask questions about what's going on, predict what will happen next, and so on. Remember – this is a discussion – not a quiz!

- The elementary school children are now beginning to pay attention to current events, so this is a good age at which to introduce junior versions of magazines such as "Sports Illustrated for Kids," "Ranger Rick," or "National Geographic Kids." Using a variety of genres (literature, magazines, newspapers, letters) shows the students the many choices of reading they have.

- Going one step further, if the children have a copy of the text and can follow along with the teacher, this provides one more skill and strategy for effective reading.

- Use whatever materials you can get your hands on for reading aloud, such as menus, signs, flyers, brochures, mail order catalogs, T-shirts, cereal boxes, and many other everyday items.

Preteens and Teens

- Just because they're older doesn't mean that pre-teens and teens don't want to be read to. To the contrary, this age group continues to associate reading with warm, pleasant feelings, and is still learning about words and language.

- Their listening skills continue to grow as they listen more intently and critically.

- Their expanded vocabulary enables them to talk more openly about characters, setting and plot of a story, as well as how they (the students) relate to them.

- This age group is becoming more aware of social and moral issues and behaviors, and gains more knowledge about a variety of topics.

- They are becoming more skilful as independent readers, are more motivated to read on their own and seek authors and writing styles that they like to read.

- They are now establishing a lifelong commitment to reading, so choosing books and material they like and are interested in is imperative.

- Consider reading editorials and articles from newspapers and magazines to maintain their interest in local, national and international current events.

- Novels set in the past and present, with young characters experiencing and coping with challenges of growing up, give the preteens and teens insights and awareness of who they are, what makes them unique and how they fit in the world.

- At this age, the students question authority, and find that the classics and modern novels that deal with "big" issues, such as the needs of a community are more important than those of individuals, are instrumental in their personal thinking and growth.

- As preteens and teens strive for independence, they're caught between being independent and maintaining a connection to their families. Read them your favorites and explain why they're important to you.

- As you read aloud, select books that challenge them to think "out of the box" and see the world beyond their own daily experiences.

- They're now gradually learning to think abstractly and understand the reasons behind views that differ from their own, so nurture this with appropriate read aloud materials.

- At this point in their lives, these students are beginning to think about what they will do with their lives, but the choices are overwhelming. Select material that introduces a wide range of opportunities and experiences, to provide a basis from which to pursue future endeavors.

<u>Reading to Students in Secondary Grades</u>

- Students don't automatically understand what they're reading just because they know how to say the words on the page – especially when the material gets complicated.

- Every subject taught in middle and/or high school, is enhanced through reading aloud by the teacher, as opposed to read and discuss or lecture methods.

- By incorporating reading aloud into content area classes, struggling readers can more readily meet with success.

- Read aloud/think aloud – reading aloud a difficult portion, then modeling "think aloud" ploys – inspire curiosity and questions, make predictions, describe mental images, draw analogies, verbalize confusing points, and provide explanations.

- "Think aloud" models a way to revisit concepts, share thinking processes and improve lagging comprehension.

- Don't overlook reading picture books aloud to engage adolescents in learning. These are highly effective as supplemental material for content-area reading. These informational books present factual knowledge, exposes students to the expository text structure, creates a desire to gain more information, and hopefully leads to independent reading of non-fiction material by students.

Reading Aloud in Specialized Subjects

Other than using picture books, here are a few suggestions to help launch you into the reading aloud mode, but the list is by no means complete. Use your creativity and discover additional ways to use reading aloud.

Science

- Anything from reading aloud the steps in a classroom experiment, to reading excerpts from magazines and newspapers that relate the latest scientific findings and breakthroughs in space travel, archeological digs, animal behavior, nature, medical science, ecology, and all other science-related information.

- Don't forget science-related literature – both fiction and non-fiction, which stimulate the mind and motivate students to learn more.

- Reading information about scientists and their discoveries from biographies and autobiographies.

- In today's world of rapidly changing scientific knowledge, teachers often feel uncomfortable teaching science (they're <u>not</u> experts in the field). They turn to read aloud material to complement the curriculum and help students make a connection between their knowledge, the textbook, their own questions, and what's happening in today's world.

Social Studies and Geography

- Relating current articles about countries, other cultures, and geographical phenomena present updated and pertinent information to the curriculum.

- Once again, reading aloud from informational sources supports students as they make connections between content and the real world.

- When picture books are incorporated into social studies classes, students, especially those with limited English, or learning disabilities, are noted, and are very effective in introducing units of study.

- Picture books can be a powerful resource when used as part of a social studies curriculum, not only to nurture an understanding of the content, but also to reinforce language arts skills.

- Again, reading from biographies or autobiographies provides insights and information in an interesting manner.

History

- Newspaper and magazine articles serve as recordings of daily historical events, which can be related to past historical events.

- Books are constantly being published that give insights to history – past and present – that hold deeper meaning and understanding for the students when they are read aloud to them.

- History trade books, when read aloud, help students connect on an aesthetic level enabling them to better remember the historical facts. Through reading aloud, students gain a deeper understanding of the content material.

- Reading picture books can increase the level of student understanding of the historical event, and of curriculum standards.

- Reading from biographies and autobiographies again provides a strong background for the people who helped create history.

English/Literature

- This is an obvious given! A read aloud from a Shakespearean play does more for Shakespeare and his writing style than any other means of teaching Shakespeare.

- The same holds true for any playwright, author, writing style, poetry or literary work.

- Some teachers may prefer to read aloud an entire book, chapter by chapter, while other teachers may prefer to pre-select portions that would serve as examples.

- Reading synopses from the literary journals of current works might motivate students to select and read independently.

- When picture books are used for reading aloud, students gain a foundation for writing skills, thus enhancing their literacy development.

Mathematics

- Problem solving from real life is quick and easy when an obituary or sports scores are read aloud. Students can calculate life spans, an athlete's record, and other vitals from listening to a related article.

- Don't overlook biographies of famous mathematicians – their discoveries and how they affect us today.

The Arts

- For any of the art forms – dramatics, visual arts, dance or music – reading aloud reviews, articles about the art form and/or artist, act as quick introductory material for the specific realm.

- Teachers can compare and contrast today's artists with past ones, include artistic techniques, and if desired, lead into performance and exhibition skills.

- Biographies and autobiographies of the artists should not be overlooked.

Home Economics

- From reading recipes aloud to fashion designing and everything in between in the realm of home economics (including child care), students appreciate "hearing" what they must do, and how to do it.

- Other career-orientated classes also find that reading aloud is beneficial to understanding how to properly use machinery and equipment, techniques, and skills.

Physical Education

- Hearing about outstanding players, and exciting games is more interesting than reading about them.

- And students will understand rules of a game when they are effectively read aloud.

Put Them All Together

- This is just scratching the surface on using reading aloud in the various subjects. How you, the teacher, choose to read aloud is entirely up to you.

- On whatever grade level, or in whatever subject you intend to read aloud, it is critical that you select your material carefully.

- You must first know your purpose for reading aloud: Is this to introduce a concept, topic or theme of study? Is it to provide some background or basic knowledge? Is it to introduce key vocabulary? Is it to increase comprehension skills and foster critical thinking? Is it for relaxation and entertainment? Is it to act as a role model for using reading strategies that aid in comprehension?

- Once you know what your goal for reading aloud is, you can select appropriate material from various sources, and present it by reading aloud to your students.

- The material you select should lend itself to being read aloud – Does it flow? Is it engaging? Are there stopping points to wonder aloud? Does it inspire questions?

- If possible, locate relevant artifacts, illustrations and other books that could support the text and make other connections to the same subject.

CHAPTER 5

Where to Read Aloud

Where to read aloud often depends upon many constraints that may, or may not, be changed. The size of the area, number of students in the classroom and physical layout of the furniture might dictate where the reading aloud can take place.

Informal Gathering – Young children in preschool and early elementary programs enjoy sitting on the floor (usually on carpeting or mats) near the teacher, who traditionally sits on a chair while reading a picture book or story. Even older elementary students enjoy this informal approach to reading aloud, where they can focus on the material being read, and are close to the teacher.

Small Groups – In some instances, students can be in a small group sitting on chairs in a circle, or around a table, or perhaps just sitting on the floor similar to the informal gathering. The group might number anywhere from 3 to 10, and might consist of a select group of students from the class, or possibly represent the class size itself, as in specialized classes.

<u>Students Remain at Their Desks</u> – For quick reading alouds, such as articles, snippets, a paragraph or two, it is often easier for the students to remain seated at their desks, rather than move to a location for a short period of time, and then return to their seats.

<u>Roaming Teacher</u> – Students remain at their desks, while the teacher reads as she walks around the perimeter of the room, between desks, up and down rows, etc. There is no special pattern, but it is interesting to note that as the teacher gets near a student, that individual becomes more attentive to the reading. When appropriate, the teacher will stop to show illustrations, ask a question, or make a comment.

<u>Opportunity Spots</u> – On occasion students might be waiting for a guest to arrive in the classroom, or waiting in line to go to lunch, an assembly program or recess. Seize the opportunity – grab a book (or article or poem) and read aloud. This is not only productive, but can eliminate discipline problems as well. Another opportunity often overlooked is while on a field trip, where students are seated on a bus or in a van. Often these vehicles have a PA system, which the teacher can use to read aloud.

If no such system is available, the teacher can read aloud short, selected material to several small groups throughout the trip. If the bus is not overcrowded, the teacher can sit on a seat, with a child on either side, and read a short picture book or poem. Then, move to another seat, and read the same material to a new group of children, until all of the children have heard the read aloud selection.

Try various places for your reading aloud, and see what works well for you and your class. It isn't necessary to always read aloud the same way and from the same spot. Variety can enhance your reading aloud program!

CHAPTER 6

Preparing to Read Aloud

Thus far, I've referred to reading aloud many times. You should have a sense about what reading aloud is, the value of reading aloud in class, what can be read aloud, and when and where to read aloud.

However, reading aloud does not come naturally. It is more than <u>just</u> reading words out loud. It requires preparation, techniques, strategies, and some do's and don'ts to keep in mind. Practicing will make reading aloud much more comfortable, and eventually it will become easier to do. Remember: You are a role model for reading! Your effectiveness in reading aloud will put students on the road to successful reading – not just while in school, but for life.

<u>Get Yourself Ready</u>

- Select appropriate material to meet your needs and goals, as well as being appropriate for the students. Choose books that are above the students' reading level, but at their interest level.

- Determine when, how and where you'll use this material.

- Quietly read through the selection to yourself – become familiar with the content, and vocabulary.

- Note areas that you'll want to emphasize, explain, ask for questions, what you might need to modify – adapt, shorten or expand.

- Read the material again – this time out loud to yourself. Mark (with post-its) specific areas or words you want to explain or emphasize.

- If possible, record (on audio tape) your reading – check for the read aloud strategies.

- Warm up your mouth muscles – stretch your mouth from side to side, and up and down. Wiggle your tongue in various directions makes your mouth and tongue more flexible, thus easier for you to read.

- While moving your mouth, make sounds too. Using individual vowels and consonants, say each one quietly at first, getting louder and louder – but not screaming.

- Reverse your volume – say your sounds loudly and gradually work your way back to quiet.

- Plan your introduction – link to students' personal experiences, introduce the title, author, illustrator, and any basic information that will facilitate understanding.

- Finally, set a purpose for listening – an "I wonder" statement.

- Get in the mood of the story or material you intend to read – Serious? Funny? Exciting? Mysterious? Unusual?

Become Expressive

Your voice is the primary tool for reading aloud – use it effectively! Don't be afraid to be a ham – the more enthusiasm you show, the more your students will enjoy listening to you read. Try these vocal exercises and discover what you can do with your voice.

1. Take a single word (Oh, Ah) and say it as a question, as thought the light bulb just went on, with disappointment, in surprise, with sadness, anger, frustration, concern, joy, etc. Use different volume levels as well. Select your own word, and say it while changing volume levels, pitch, pace, inflections and intonations. Note how each interpretation gives a different image or feeling.

2. Now do the same exercise only this time use a complete phrase such as "I don't understand why I have to do this." Emphasize the first word (I_don't understand, etc.) Say the phrase again, this time emphasizing the second word (I don't understand, etc.) Keep repeating the phrase, each time placing emphasis on the next word. Note how the meaning of the phrase changes as the inflections and intonations change.

3. Using the material you plan to read, try these exercises to discover the expressions you wish to use.

4. Give your voice variation in pitches – range from high to low. If you're reading as a character, picture the character and use a voice that would be appropriate, such as a deep voice for a big character; or a high pitch for a small character.

5. Vary your volume levels – a loud voice is appropriate when reading something exciting or showing anger; a soft voice is appropriate for quiet scenes, timid characters, secrecy, or showing fear.

6. Let your voice move in various rhythms, rather than one pattern. Variation makes the reading more interesting to the listener.

7. Vary your pacing – reading rapidly works well to show excitement or highly charged emotions and reactions; slower reading is effective for calm, serene portions, and allows the words to "sink in".

8. Pausing before reading something important allows the listener to "jump in" to the story or material, in an attempt to "second guess" what will be said next. This "pause for effect" is a valuable tool for listening and for re-focusing the listener who may have "drifted away." As you "practice" your material, locate places where the pause for effect can be used.

9. Use your voice for sound effects, if they fit into your material. Practice chirping like a bird, making animal sounds, hissing like a snake, roaring like a machine, and so on. Sounds incorporated into your reading make the piece more meaningful and memorable to the student.

10. As you read, relax! Remember to breathe easily – deeply from the diaphragm. Before starting, take a deep breath, and slowly exhale as you read. This gives you the breath you need so your reading is smooth, and not broken with taking a breath, hems or haws.

11. Finally, always keep in mind that the words read should be clear and distinct, the volume level (even while speaking softly) should be sufficient so the students can hear what you're saying, and for the most part, your pacing should be slow enough to allow for comprehension.

During Reading – Other Factors to Consider

1. Use facial expressions that fit what you're saying, as well as the emotions or mood of the piece being read.

2. Use gestures and body movements (hands, arms, legs and feet) that are natural and meaningful to what you're reading. Be cautious of using gestures randomly.

3. Periodically, look up from your material and scan your students. Are they looking at you and listening? Are they reacting to what you are reading?

4. When you do look up, try to make eye contact with one or more students. This provides feedback for you, and also makes the student feel as though you are reading just to him!

CHAPTER 7

Reading Aloud in Action

Now you're ready to put your strategies and skills to work – you're all set to actually read aloud to your class.

You've prepared yourself by finding the appropriate material to read; you've read it through to know what expressiveness you'll use and where you'll pause; you've practiced reading the material aloud to yourself so you are comfortable with it; you're aware of the various strategies to use as discussed in the previous chapter.

Although you, the teacher, are doing the reading, reading aloud is really an interactive process. You read; students listen and respond. However, to wait for their responses until the reading is over can negate the value of reading aloud. Initially, you've introduced the material and invited predictions and personal connections.

Now, your class is ready to listen (you've made sure of that!) You pick up your material, provide your introduction, and begin to read from material you are properly holding in your hands - in front of you. It has been noted that many teachers of young children hold the book off to one side, or read the book upside down. This is not proper modeling for reading a book!

During Reading

- For young children, they may be invited to supply sound effects, chants, or repeated phrases that appear in a story. However, if this interaction is what you want, you will need to introduce what you want the children to say or do before you read the story. The children will listen for "their part" and will be ready.

- Read fluently and expressively and establish eye contact where possible.

- Draw attention to illustrations and special features of the material you want the children to be aware of.

- Pause occasionally to review predictions, express curiosity, or make comments.

- Invite questions, comments or predictions about the text or illustrations – CAUTION: Keep this to a minimum so you don't lose focus on the material being read.

- If necessary, explain words or concepts the students might not understand.

- Feel free to add information or change words for better understanding.

- Repeat words or phrases to make sure the students grasp them.

- Constantly scan the students – be sensitive to signs of boredom or confusion and be aware of their attention span and interest to determine how long you should read.

- If you need to stop reading, select a suspenseful or interesting point that will encourage the students to want to hear more at a later time. When you resume the reading, summarize what was previously read.

- If you need to stop reading because the students are not interested, be honest – admit this was not a good selection, and you'll find something better for next time.
- Don't rush through a story to finish it. Longer stories can be read over several sessions, but keep the time between readings short and stop at good places.

After Reading

- Allow time for discussion through direct or open-ended questions, where there are no right or wrong answers.
- It's the talk that surrounds the reading that gives it power by helping students to bridge what is in the story and their own lives.
- Allow students to make personal connections to the text – "What did this remind you of?" "Have you ever had a similar experience?" "How did you feel about this?"
- Allow students to express personal reactions – "What was your favorite part, and why?" "What part did you like least and why?" "Describe one of the characters and how they might feel or act if they were that character?"
- Feel free to share your own reactions and thinking about the story, special language patterns or phrases that made you visualize something.
- Ask students what they learned from this reading. Ask what they thought the author was trying to tell them.
- Encourage students to retell (in their own words) the story, or summarize the material presented.
- Extend the story or material read to other activities or other books.

Some Basic Tips to Remember

- DO preview your book/material and read it to yourself.

- DO find time every day to read aloud to your students.

- DO start with picture books and build to novels – with other materials in between.

- DO vary your expression, intonations, pacing, volume and levels to suit the story or material being read.

- DO vary the type and length of material you read aloud.

- DO read at a speed that will give the students a chance to absorb and understand what you're reading.

- DO allow time before and after reading to talk about the book, reactions, comments, questions, and personal feelings.

- DON'T read stories or material that you yourself don't enjoy or find interesting.

- DON'T continue to read if your students appear restless. More is not always best.

- DON'T continue reading once it's obvious that it was a poor choice. Admit the mistake and choose something else.

- DON'T be unnerved by questions during the reading. Patiently respond to them, and then resume reading so the focus isn't lost.

- DON'T confuse quantity with quality. Reading aloud (even if it's short) for 5 minutes is better than not reading aloud at all.

- DON'T use reading aloud as a threat – "If you don't do this, then I won't read to you today." Using books as a weapon is likely to change a child's attitude toward books from positive to negative.

CHAPTER 8

Reading Aloud Is for Everyone

According to a statement made in *Becoming a Nation of Readers,* by *the Commission on Reading,* "The single most important activity for building knowledge for their eventual success in reading is reading aloud to children."

How Students Benefit

Over and over, where reading aloud to children is integrated into the classroom, children have displayed positive results. Besides being 'fun', it is a source of pleasant, valuable and exciting experiences. Children who are read aloud to see that a book is read from front to back and there is a difference between pictures and print. They recognize the relationship between the written word and knowledge, and are motivated to want to read on their own.

In a warm, relaxed, and supportive environment, students listen intently to their teachers reading aloud. As listening skills build, so do comprehension skills through discussion during and after the reading. They absorb and expand their vocabularies by hearing words used in context. The more they listen and hear stories and information, their memory improves, as does their ability to paraphrase, and their understanding of the various writing styles they have heard increases.

Listening to reading aloud helps students gain knowledge and information about the world around them, and in areas that might otherwise be out of their reach. Teachers who read aloud introduce books and material that students might not discover on their own. Through the teacher's read aloud choices, students develop their own individual interests in a broad variety of subjects, while simultaneously developing their imagination and creativity.

A teacher's enthusiasm while reading aloud is contagious! As they listen to the reading, students use their imaginations to explore people, places, times and events. They hear how words are used – the descriptive and grammatical uses for language that they'll eventually put to use in their own creative writing endeavors.

After the reading aloud is over, students have the opportunity to express themselves through discussions, relating what they have heard to their own lives. Reading aloud supports the development of critical thinking skills, and students can extend their own thinking about themselves and the world in which they live.

Reading loud brings a book, article, play, poem, or any other written material, to life! And it's all done through the expressive reading of the teacher.

How Teachers Benefit

The words are already written for you. Teachers don't have to compose anything – all they have to do is read the written word!

Teachers don't have to prepare detailed notes or lesson plans.

Teachers have authorities in the various areas to rely on, and don't have to be the 'expert' in any field.

Teachers work with students who are better listeners and learners.

Teachers see quick results to their efforts.

Teachers feel proud of their accomplishments.

The Bottom Line

Through reading aloud, students are "turned on" to the job of reading. The more children read, the better readers they become. Students move from hearing to reading, to telling and writing stories, using the literary patterns the reading aloud exposes them to.

Now ask yourself: Did you read aloud today? Will you read aloud tomorrow? And the next day, and the day after that? Hopefully, reading aloud one or more times will become part of your daily routine in whatever grade or subject matter you teach.

AUTHOR BIO

Born in Washington. D.C, Judy wrote skits and articles throughout her school years. Upon graduation, she attended Penn State University and graduated with a BS in child development. Her first job was as an assistant home economist in Chambersburg, PA, where she wrote a column in the local newspaper. The following year, Judy was hired as a 4-H club director in Montgomery County, MD. She left that job to marry Al Wolfe, a disc jockey working in Altoona, PA, where they raised two boys before moving to Wilkes-Barre, PA, where her daughter was born. Three years later, the family moved to York, PA, where they lived for forty years. Judy accepted a job with the York City School District as a pre-K teacher until her retirement after thirty years. She then turned to writing and published twenty books and seventeen plays. After Al's death, Judy moved to Country Meadows, a retirement community in York, where she currently lives.

www.ingramcontent.com/pod-product-compliance
Lightning Source LLC
Chambersburg PA
CBHW072140150726
48002CB00004B/1561